KB090380

Get Real!

Discussion and Debate

for English Language Learners

Myeong-Hee Seong
Katie Mae Klemsen

BAEKSAN
Publishing Co

C·o·n·t·e·n·t·s

C·o·n·t·e·n·t·s

Unit 1

Black as Night, Hot as Hell

Get Real!
Discussion and Debate
for English Language Learners

Unit 01 Black as Night, Hot as Hell

📂 Vocabulary Preview

Conclusion	Rich	Source	Antioxidants
Provider	Caffeine	Frequency	Auxiliary
Uptake	To stress (verb)	Diuretic	Purge
Dehydrated	Benefits	Caffeinated	Decaffeinated
Consumption	Blood pressure	Disrupt	Diet

Coffee Provides Antioxidants

Coffee is good for you. That is the conclusion of researchers at the University of Scranton in Pennsylvania. A team led by Dr. Joe Vinson found coffee is a rich source of antioxidants. Coffee is the biggest provider of these vitamins in the U.S. diet.

Antioxidants help fight cancer and reduce cell damage and the effects of aging. Dr. Vinson said both caffeinated and decaffeinated coffee provides similar levels of antioxidants. He recommended no more than two cups of coffee a day.

Vinson analyzed the antioxidant content of more than 100 different food items and beverages. Coffee finished at the top, based on serving size and frequency of consumption. However, Vinson advised people not to think of coffee as a health drink. He stressed that high antioxidant levels in coffee does not mean the vitamins will find their way into our bodies.

Some vitamins need auxiliary vitamins to increase uptake. For example, calcium needs vitamin D in order to be absorbed into the body. No amount of coffee or caffeine can substitute for this.

The dangers of coffee are that it causes stomach pains, increases blood pressure and can lead to heart problems. Too much caffeine can disrupt sleep patterns. In addition, caffeine acts as a diuretic, purging the body of excess water. If someone takes in too much caffeine, from coffee or other sources, they run the risk of becoming dehydrated.

Vinson said more research is needed to understand its health benefits.

Discussion and Debate

1. Answer the following questions related to the article.

1) Do you drink coffee?

   a Why or why not?
   b If yes, how many cups a day do you drink?
   c How many cups a week do you drink?

2) Have you ever had too much coffee?

   a What happened?
   b How did you feel?

3) Does coffee play a big role in social culture?

   a Do people use coffee as a means of seeing each other?
   b Are there many coffee shops where you live?

4) Is coffee expensive?

   a How much does the average beverage cost?
   b Is it worth the money?

5) Why do you like or dislike coffee?

   a What about the taste?
   b What about the smell?
   c What about the café atmosphere?

6) Do you put sweetener in your coffee?

> [a] Do you use sugar?
> [b] Do you use milk?
> [c] Do you use a non-dairy creamer?
> [d] Do you use a low-calorie substitute?

7) Do coffee farmers get a fair price for their product?

> [a] What do you know about coffee farming?
> [b] What do you know about fair-trade coffee?

8) Is coffee healthy?

> [a] How many calories does a cup of black coffee have?
> [b] What about a latte?
> [c] What about a mocha?
> [d] Are there hidden calories in some coffee beverages?
> [e] What is the healthiest coffee beverage option?

9) What are some of the possible negative effects of drinking coffee?

> [a] What about blood pressure?
> [b] What about dehydration?
> [c] What about caffeine dependency?
> [d] What happens if you suddenly stop drinking coffee daily?

10) Is coffee the best way to get the antioxidants the body needs?

> [a] What other foods or beverages do you know of that have a lot of antioxidants?
> [b] Do you think about nutrients and antioxidants when you choose a food or drink?

Building Vocabulary

1. Review this list of vocabulary words. Translate the English words into Korean.

► English	►► Korean	► English	►► Korean
Conclusion		Diuretic	
Rich		Purge	
Source		Dehydrated	
Antioxidants		Benefits	
Provider		Caffeinated	
Caffeine		Decaffeinated	
Frequency		Consumption	
Auxiliary		Blood pressure	
Uptake		Disrupt	
To stress (verb)		Diet	

2. Which words from part 1 match the following synonyms?

1) Supporting:

2) Plentiful:

3) Dried out:

4) Flush out:

5) Absorption:

3. Seek the words. Find the vocabulary words from the box below in the puzzle.

Conclusion	Rich Source	Antioxidants	Provider	Caffeine
Frequency	Auxiliary	Uptake	Stress	Diuretic
Purge	Dehydrated	Benefits	Caffeinated	Decaffeinated
Consumption	Blood pressure	Disrupt	Diet	

Coffee Is Good for You													
D	I	U	R	E	T	I	C	B	D	E	J	D	N	R
E	C	R	U	O	S	Y	S	L	E	K	N	L	O	E
F	B	P	E	D	U	S	Q	O	C	A	U	G	I	D
D	P	E	U	E	E	S	F	O	A	T	L	G	T	I
F	R	X	N	R	M	T	G	D	F	P	V	F	P	V
R	E	X	T	E	G	K	A	E	F	U	N	M	M	O
E	S	S	H	R	F	E	N	N	E	O	F	V	U	R
Q	S	T	N	A	D	I	X	O	I	T	N	A	S	P
U	U	Y	W	R	E	D	T	S	N	E	R	Z	N	K
E	R	Y	I	F	I	E	U	S	A	H	F	D	O	W
N	E	C	F	S	E	L	K	V	T	Z	M	F	C	N
C	H	A	R	L	C	P	J	T	E	I	D	V	A	V
Y	C	U	O	N	J	M	J	C	D	U	I	U	B	C
F	P	J	O	S	D	E	H	Y	D	R	A	T	E	D
T	F	C	Y	R	A	I	L	I	X	U	A	K	I	T

Practice Makes Perfect

1. Read the following statements about the article. Answer true or false.

    a)   A new study concludes that coffee is good for you.   T / F

    b)   Coffee provides the biggest source of antioxidants for   T / F
        Americans.

    c)   Antioxidants lead to cancer.   T / F

    d)   Decaffeinated coffee has more antioxidants than caffeinated   T / F
        coffee.

    e)   A study compared 100 different types of coffee.   T / F

    f)   A researcher said coffee should be thought of as a health   T / F
        drink.

    g)   Antioxidants from coffee are quickly absorbed in our bodies.   T / F

    h)   Coffee can increase blood pressure.   T / F

2. Circle the correct word or words from the article.

Coffee is good for you. That is the *concussion / conclusion* of researchers at the University of Scranton in Pennsylvania. A team *led / fled* by Dr. Joe Vinson found coffee is a rich *sour / source* of antioxidants. Coffee is the biggest provider of these vitamins in the U.S. *diet / dietician*. Antioxidants help fight cancer and reduce cell damage and the effects of *agreeing / aging*. Dr. Vinson said both caffeinated and decaffeinated coffee provides *simultaneous / similar* levels of antioxidants. He recommended no more than two cups of coffee a day.

3. With a partner, decide if coffee is a good beverage for the following activities.

• A date	• On a cold day
• While reading	• On a hot day
• While driving	• To sleep early
• While studying	• To stay up all night

NOTES:

Write On!

Free write for 10 minutes about coffee. Be creative! What words do you think of when you think of coffee? What kind of coffee do you like? Do you prefer tea to coffee?

📝 Phrasal Verbs

To ward off

- It helps ward off cancer.
- It helps ward it off.
- He should ward off _____.

The Whole Story

Read these fascinating facts related to coffee.

---------------------------- Coffee Facts ----------------------------

① The word coffee was originally Arabic and means "excitement."

② Coffee was discovered in Ethiopia, a country located in Africa.

③ Coffee is the second most traded product in the world after petroleum.

④ One coffee tree produces just 1/2 kilo of roasted coffee.

⑤ Brazil is the largest coffee-producing nation. It produces 40% of the total world output.

⑥ Over 53 countries grow coffee worldwide.

⑦ We use the term "coffee beans" even though they come from berries. Each coffee berry has two beans.

⑧ 27% of U.S. coffee drinkers and 43% of German drinkers add a sweetener to their coffee.

⑨ October 1st is the official Coffee Day in Japan.

⑩ 25 million families around the world work in coffee fields.

NOTES:

Unit
2

Decoding Color

Get Real!
Discussion and Debate
for English Language Learners

Unit 02 — Decoding Color

⏻ Themes and Topics

- Attraction
- Color
- Psychology
- Dating
- Human relationships
- Sex and pop culture

🗁 Vocabulary Preview

Attractive	Suggest	Conduct	Experiment
Human relationships		Score	Rate
Details	Expensive	Data	Psychology
Fascinating	Ever-present	Behavior	Awareness
Informal	Expressions	Seeing red	Feeling blue
Popularity			

Red is Hot, Hot, Hot!

Why can a person be more attractive one day and seem less attractive another? A new study suggests that men are more physically attracted to a woman if she wears red clothes.

The report from New York's University of Rochester conducted different experiments to find out the effects of color on human relationships. Researchers asked more than 100 men to give a score to photographs of women. The men had to rate the women according to how pretty they were, how much the men would like to kiss them, their intelligence and how kind they looked. They also had to provide details of what kind of date they would like to take the women on.

The results showed that the women in the pictures who wore red scored higher and were more likely to be taken on an expensive date. The data showed the color red made no impact on the scores for intelligence and kindness It seems that wearing red can make a woman seem sexier, but not more or less intelligent.

Psychology professor Andrew Elliot and his team carried out the research. Professor Elliot said he found it fascinating to find that something as ever-present as color can be having an effect on our behavior without our awareness.

This is one of the first scientific studies to look at the effects of color on human behavior. More informal studies have shown that if a person uses a blue colored plate, he or she will eat less. Many expressions, such as "seeing red", which means to be angry, or "feeling blue", which means one is sad or feeling depressed, show the impact of color on English speaking cultures around the world.

For most of us, however, it will come as no surprise that women in red seem more attractive; red is the color of love and passion. Look no further than red roses on Valentine's Day and the popularity of deep red lipsticks. Elliot says men may be genetically programmed to be attracted to females wearing red. He said certain apes also display such behavior.

Women involved in the study did not rate the pictured females as prettier, nor did they have the chance to rate men wearing different colors.

NOTES:

Discussion and Debate

1. Answer the following questions related to the article.

1) What is sexy?

   a Is it a physical quality or an internal quality?

   b Is it the same for men and women? How is it similar or different?

   c What makes someone seem more or less attractive?

2) Are the standards for attractiveness the same for men and women?

   a Who has higher standards of beauty? Why?

   b Are high standards of beauty encouraging plastic surgery?

3) If women seem more attractive wearing the color red, what do other colors say about women?

   a Blue

   b Black

   c White

   d Yellow

4) Do you feel differently when you wear red, blue, white or any other color?

   a Which color makes you happy?

   b Which color do you think of when you think of the winter season?

   c Which color represents summer?

5) Discuss the significance of color in clothing in your culture.

   a What color do you wear to a wedding or a funeral?

   b What would happen if you went against those cultural norms?

6) In most cultures pink is for girls and blue is for boys. Discuss color and gender identification.

   a Is it a good idea to associate babies with a sense of masculinity or femininity?

   b Should people dress babies in gender-specific clothing?

   c How would you dress a 2-year-old girl?

   d How would you dress a 2-year-old boy?

7) How can color be used to your advantage? Discuss:

   a Job interviews

   b Dating

   c Traditional culture

   d Pop culture

8) Do you agree with the findings in this study?

   a Why or why not?

   b Do you think that women in red seem more attractive?

9) What is the relationship between the changing concept of attractiveness and the sexual nature of popular advertisements on television and print?

   a Are advertisements sexual?

   b Does sex sell?

   c Does the desire to "be and feel sexy" make people buy and use products they might otherwise not use?

10) If you are a woman, are the results of this study going to affect when and how often you wear the color red?

   a Why or why not?

   b How could you use this information to your advantage or disadvantage?

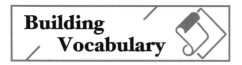

Building Vocabulary

1. Review this list of vocabulary words. Translate the English words into Korean.

▶ English	▶▶ Korean	▶ English	▶▶ Korean
Attractive		Psychology	
Suggest		Fascinating	
Conduct		Ever-present	
Experiment		Behavior	
Human relationships		Awareness	
Score		Informal	
Rate		Expressions	
Details		Seeing red	
Expensive		Feeling blue	
Data		Popularity	

2. Use the following words from part 1 in a sentence.

1) Fascinating:

2) Details:

3) Suggest:

4) Attractive:

5) Popularity:

3. Pair Work. Use the information in part 2 to practice with your partner.

4. What features do you find attractive in a partner? Complete the table below. Score each feature from 1 (not at all important) to 10 (essential).

Feature	1 ~ 10	Why?
Looks		
Body shape		
Clothes		
Intelligence		
Money		
Humor		
Kindness		

Practice Makes Perfect

1. Read the following statements about the article. Answer true or false.

a) Men prefer women who wear red clothes.   T / F

b) Part of a study was for men to kiss an intelligent woman in a red dress.   T / F

c) A study said men might spend more on a date if the woman wore red.   T / F

d) Men said that women who wore yellow were kind.   T / F

e) The researcher said we are very aware of how color affects us.   T / F

f) Few people would be surprised that red is the color of passion.   T / F

g) Male apes prefer female apes that wear red.   T / F

h) Women were more attracted to men who wear different colors.   T / F

2. Fill in the following blanks with words or phrases from the article.

A new study suggests that men are more _____ attracted to a woman if she wears red clothes. The report from New York's University of Rochester conducted _____ experiments to find out the effects of color on human relationships. Researchers asked more than 100 men to give a _____ to photographs of women. The men had to _____ the women according to how pretty they were, how much the men would like to kiss them, their intelligence and how kind they _____. They also had to provide details of what kind of date they would like to _____ the women on. The results showed that the women in the pictures who wore red scored higher and were more _____ to be taken on an expensive date. The data showed the color red made no _____ on the scores for intelligence and kindness.

3. With a partner, discuss which color is best suited for the following:

• A woman's dress	• Nail polish
• A man's suit	• A library
• A computer	• A car
• Chocolate	• A sports shirt

Write On!

Free write for 10 minutes about the color red. Be creative! What words come to mind when you think of the color red?

NOTES:

The Whole Story

Read these fascinating facts related to color.

Black: Black is the color of authority and power. It is popular in fashion because it makes people appear thinner. It is also stylish and timeless. Black also implies submission. Priests wear black to signify submission to God. Some fashion experts say a woman wearing black implies submission to men. Black outfits can also be overpowering, or make the wearer seem aloof or evil. Villains, such as Dracula, often wear black.

White: Brides wear white to symbolize innocence and purity. White reflects light and is considered a summer color. White is popular in decorating and in fashion because it is light, neutral, and goes with everything. However, white shows dirt and is therefore more difficult to keep clean than other colors. Doctors and nurses wear white to imply sterility.

Red: The most emotionally intense color, red stimulates a faster heartbeat and breathing. It is also the color of love. Red clothing gets noticed and makes the wearer appear heavier. Since it is an extreme color, red clothing might not help people in negotiations or confrontations. Red cars are popular targets for thieves. In decorating, red is usually used as an accent. Decorators say that red furniture should be perfect since it will attract attention.

Pink: The most romantic color, pink, is more tranquilizing. Sports teams sometimes paint the locker rooms used by opposing teams bright pink so their opponents will lose energy.

Blue: The color of the sky and the ocean, blue is one of the most popular colors. It causes the opposite reaction as red. Peaceful, tranquil blue causes the body to produce calming chemicals, so it is often used in bedrooms. Blue can also be cold and depressing. Fashion consultants recommend wearing blue to job interviews because it symbolizes loyalty. People are more productive in blue rooms. Studies show weightlifters are able to handle heavier weights in blue gyms.

Green: Currently the most popular decorating color, green symbolizes nature. It is the easiest color on the eye and can improve vision. It is a calming, refreshing color. People waiting to appear on TV sit in "green rooms" to relax. Hospitals often use green because it relaxes patients. Brides in the Middle Ages wore green to symbolize fertility. Dark green is masculine, conservative, and implies wealth. However, seamstresses often refuse to use green thread on the eve of a fashion show for fear it will bring bad luck.

Yellow: Cheerful sunny yellow is an attention getter. While it is considered an optimistic color, people lose their tempers more often in yellow rooms, and babies will cry more. It is the most difficult color for the eye to take in, so it can be overpowering if overused. Yellow enhances concentration, hence its use for legal pads. It also speeds metabolism.

Purple: The color of royalty, purple connotes luxury, wealth, and sophistication. It is also feminine and romantic. However, because it is rare in nature, purple can appear artificial.

Brown: Solid, reliable brown is the color of earth and is abundant in nature. Light brown implies genuineness while dark brown is similar to wood or leather. Brown can also be sad and wistful. Men are more apt to say brown is one of their favorite colors.

Unit
3

A Small but Bright Light

Get Real!
Discussion and Debate
for English Language Learners

Unit 03 — A Small but Bright Light

Themes and Topics

- God
- Religion
- Humanity
- Spirituality

Vocabulary Preview

Faith	Major	Follower	Progressive
Revelation	Independent	Distinct	Pillar
Relatively	Founded	Administrative	Rituals
Dogmatic	Discouraged	Gatherings	Empowerment
Humanitarian	Development	Humanity	Collective
Inheritance	Systematically	Consciously	Responsibility

The Baha'i Faith Offers a New Perspective

The Baha'i Faith is a major world religion with more than 5 million followers. They believe in progressive revelation, which is the revealing of the word of God over time. It is an independent religion and not a sect or a part of any other religion. There are no priests, pastors or ministers. It is practiced in 127,400 distinct geographic locations, including Korea, and in 802 languages. Its pillars are the oneness of God, man and religion.

The faith is a relatively new one, having been founded by Baha'u'llah in the middle of 19th century in Persia, which is now Iran and Iraq. Baha'u'llah is a title given to the founder and is made up of two words: "Baha," meaning glory and "Allah," meaning God. Baha'u'llah is "the Glory of God."

Baha'is worship daily, in their homes and regularly hold prayer gatherings in their administrative center. There are no rituals; dogmatic practices are discouraged.

The Baha'i community is open to everyone and welcomes people from any race or religion to participate in gatherings, prayer meetings and important festivals. They also study the Baha'i Writings and plan programs to serve the outer community in child education, junior youth empowerment and humanitarian community services aimed at spiritual, social and educational development.

According to the Baha'is, humanity has entered a new era of enlightenment and all people are now challenged to draw on their collective inheritance, to take up the responsibility consciously and systematically, for the design of the future.

Discussion and Debate

1. Answer the following questions related to the article.

1) Do you believe in God?

   a Why or why not?
   b How many Gods are there?
   c Do you have any evidence that God exists?

2) Does each religion have its own God?

   a Are religions separate?
   b Do all religions believe in the same God?

3) Why do humans seek a connection with "God"?

   a Are we born spiritual?
   b Are we taught to become spiritual?

4) Is belief in God the same as being religious?

   a What is the difference between acknowledging God and being religious?
   b Do you have to believe in God to be a good person?
   c Do you have to be religious to be a good person?

5) What is the purpose of religion?

   a Is it to know God?
   b Is it to know ourselves?
   c Is it to judge others that are unlike us?

d Is it to learn about virtues?

e Is it to go to heaven?

6) What does it mean to be "spiritual"?

a Does it mean to connect to a higher power?

b Does it mean to connect to humanity?

c Does it mean to develop your potential?

d Does it mean to turn away from organized religion?

7) Where do we come from?

a God?

b Our parents?

c The soul of the universe?

8) Where do we go when we die?

a Do we return to God?

b Do we go nowhere?

c Do we return to the Earth?

d Do we return to the soul of the universe?

9) Does humanity need religion?

a Is it good for humanity?

b Is it bad for humanity?

c Does it unite people?

d Does it divide people?

10) Is there a connection between nature and God?

   a   Where do you see God?
   b   Is God alive in nature?
   c   Can being close to nature bring us closer to God?
   d   How can we benefit from being close to God?

NOTES:

Building Vocabulary

1. Review this list of vocabulary words. Translate the English words into Korean.

▶ English	▶▶ Korean	▶ English	▶▶ Korean
Faith		Dogmatic	
Major		Discouraged	
Follower		Gatherings	
Progressive		Empowerment	
Revelation		Humanitarian	
Independent		Development	
Distinct		Humanity	
Pillar		Collective	
Relatively		Inheritance	
Founded		Systematically	
Administrative		Consciously	
Rituals		Responsibility	

2. Match the following synonyms with vocabulary words from part 1.

1) Legacy:

2) Expansion:

3) Custom:

4) Forward moving:

5) Deliberately:

```
┌─────────────────────────┐
│  Practice Makes          │
│      Perfect             │
└─────────────────────────┘
```

1. Read the following statements about the article. Answer true or false.

a)	The Baha'i Faith is a new world religion.	T / F
b)	The Baha'i Faith is practiced in 208 languages.	T / F
c)	Baha'i is a sect of Islam.	T / F
d)	Baha'is encourage new and flexible practices in their faith.	T / F
e)	Baha'is go to church.	T / F
f)	The Baha'is have no pastors.	T / F
g)	Baha'is believe in the oneness of God, man and religion.	T / F
h)	They support social and economic development in their communities.	T / F

2. What do you know about the following religions? Discuss them with a partner.

• Christianity	• Zorastorism
• Islam	• Catholicism
• Buddhism	• Wicca
• Hindu	• Mormon

3. Fill in the following chart with what you know about the following religions. Mark yes or no for the questions and ask your classmates if you think they have practicing members in Korea.

Religion	Pray / How?	Attend worship services	Practice in Korea?
Christianity			
Zorastorism			
Jewish			
Islam			
Mormon			
Baha'i			

NOTES:

Write On!

Free write for 10 minutes about God. Be creative! What do you know about God? What is God? Who is God? How do you feel about having a relationship with God?

_____

_____

_____

_____

_____

_____

_____

_____

_____

_____

_____

_____

_____

_____

_____

🖉 Phrasal Verbs

To make up

- I have to make it up.
- I want you to make up a story.
- Make it up!

The Whole Story

Read these fascinating facts about the Mayan culture and religion.

The Maya are a native Mesoamerican people who developed one of the most sophisticated cultures in the Western Hemisphere before the arrival of the Spanish.

Mayan religion was characterized by the worship of nature gods, especially the gods of sun, rain and corn, a priestly class, the importance of astronomy and astrology, rituals of human sacrifice, and the building of elaborate pyramid-like temples.

Some aspects of Mayan religion survive today among the Mayan Indians of Mexico and Central America, who practice a combination of traditional religion and Roman Catholicism.

Date founded:

250 AD (rise of the Maya civilization)

Place founded:

Mesoamerica (Southern Mexico, Guatemala, Belize)

Believers:

Up to 2 million. Today, several million Maya practice a Roman Catholicism that retains many elements of traditional Mayan religion.

Theism:

Polytheism, which means the belief and worship of many gods.

Practices:

Astronomy, divination, human sacrifice, elaborate burial for royalty, worship in stone pyramid-temples.

Secrets of the Mayan Calendar

The Maya practiced a form of **divination** that centered on their elaborate calendar system and extensive knowledge of astronomy. It was the job of the priests to discern lucky days from unlucky ones, and advising the rulers on the best days to plant, harvest or wage war. They were especially interested in the movements of the planet Venus and the Maya rulers scheduled wars to coordinate with its rise in the heavens.

The **Mayan calendar** was very advanced, and consisted of a solar year of 365 days. It was divided into 18 months of 20 days each, followed by a five-day period that was highly unlucky. There was also a 260-day sacred year (tzolkin), divided into days named by the combination of 13 numbers and 20 names.

NOTES:

Unit 4

The New Dangers of Drinking

Get Real!
Discussion and Debate
for English Language Learners

Unit 04

The New Dangers of Drinking

⏻ Themes and Topics

- Drinking
- Communication
- Relationships

📂 Vocabulary Preview

Regret	Search engine	Safeguard	Unusual
Handy	Application	State of mind	Novel (adjective)
Widget	Countless	Embarrassing	Situations
Default	Mistake	Prefer	To have a crush on
Potential	Brink	Regret	Prevent

Google to the Rescue

If you have ever sent an e-mail when you were drunk and then regretted it, Google has the answer for you. The search engine giant has created a new safeguard for users of its free e-mail service Gmail.

The new feature goes by the name "Mail Goggles". The unusual but handy little application, especially for drunks who have the urge to mail people, makes you answer a few simple math problems before clicking the send button. If you can't do the math, you will be asked if you're really sure you're in the right state of mind to continue. This novel widget might just help save countless relationships, jobs and other embarrassing situations. The Gmail blog says: "Hopefully Mail Goggles will prevent many of you out there from sending messages you wish you hadn't."

Mail Goggles has a default setting that means it is only active on Friday and Saturday nights between 10 p.m. and 4 a.m. This is the time when people send most angry and silly mails by mistake. Users can go to the settings in the menu bar and choose other times if they prefer. Perhaps another dangerous time to send e-mails is first thing on Monday morning.

Engineer Jon Perlow from Google Labs wrote on the Gmail blog: "Sometimes I send messages I shouldn't send. Like the time I told that girl I had a crush on her over text message. Or the time I sent that late night email to my ex-girlfriend that we should get back together."

Most circles of friends are full of stories of alcohol-fuelled mails that caused damage. Alcohol has the potential to drive anyone to the brink of sending a message they regret. Thanks to Google, we have one less thing to worry about.

Discussion and Debate

1. Answer the following questions related to the article.

1) Have you ever, or do you know someone who has, written an e-mail after drinking?

   a To whom did you or your friend write?
   b What was the nature of the e-mail?

2) Is writing an e-mail a good idea after drinking?

   a Is making a telephone call a good idea?
   b What about going to school or work?

3) What emotions can be intensified with alcohol?

   a How does this affect communication?
   b Is it better to talk about problem drunk or sober?

4) If you use Gmail, are you planning on using this application?

   a Do you think this function will be helpful to your friends of family?
   b Are you concerned you might send a drunken e-mail?
   c Do you wish you had this function on your cell phone?

5) What types of problems can this new application help avoid?

   a With a parent?
   b With a friend?
   c With a boyfriend or girlfriend?

6) Do people tend to drink more when they have problems or are experiencing more stress than normal?

  a How does this relate to e-mails?
  b How does this relate to phone calls?

7) Are people judged equally for their actions while they are drunk and while they are sober?

  a When, while drunk or sober, are actions taken more seriously?
  b Is being drunk an excuse for being foolish?

8) If a friend wrote a mean or nasty e-mail to you while he or she was drunk, how would you feel?

  a What would you do after reading the e-mail?
  b Would you call your friend?
  c Would you respond to the e-mail?
  d Would you forgive your friend?

9) What is the relationship between regrettable decisions or mistakes and drinking?

  a Is writing an e-mail the only bad thing that can happen if you drink too much?
  b What about cheating?
  c What about drinking and driving?
  d What about becoming violent?

10) How much is too much to drink?

  a Is it different for women and men?
  b Why or why not?

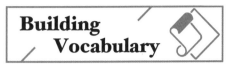

1. Review this list of vocabulary words. Translate the English words into Korean.

▸ English	▸▸ Korean	▸ English	▸▸ Korean
Regret		Embarrassing	
Search engine		Situations	
Safeguard		Default	
Unusual		Mistake	
Handy		Prefer	
Application		To have a crush on	
State of mind		Potential	
Novel (adjective)		Brink	
Widget		Regret	
Countless		Prevent	

2. Match the following definitions with vocabulary words from part 1.

   1) To fall for someone:

   2) Strange:

   3) Uncomfortable:

   4) Useful:

   5) Be remorseful:

Practice Makes Perfect

1. Read the following statements about the article. Answer true or false.

  a) New software closes an e-mail if it knows the writer is drunk. T / F

  b) The writer says the application is not particularly useful. T / F

  c) The software asks you some math problems to see if you're T / F
      with it.

  d) The new software could stop people from losing a job or T / F
      their partner.

  e) Google's new service only works on Friday and Saturday T / F
      nights.

  f) Most mails that people regret are sent on Monday mornings. T / F

  g) Alcohol can affect people's ability to communicate well. T / F

  h) Drunken people must use this new application. T / F

2. Fill in the following blanks with words or phrases from the article.

  If you have _____ e-mail when you were drunk and then
_____, Google has the answer for you. The search engine giant has
created a new safeguard for _____ free e-mail service Gmail. The
new feature goes by the name "Mail Goggles". The unusual _____
little application, especially for drunks who have the urge to mail people,
makes you pass a few simple math problems before clicking the send button.
If you can't _____, you will be asked if you're really sure you're
in the _____ mind to continue. This novel widget may

_____ countless relationships, jobs and other embarrassing situations.
The Gmail blog says: "Hopefully Mail Goggles will prevent many of you out
there from sending messages you _____."

3. Can you do damage with e-mail? Fill in the chart with different
   embarrassments that e-mails could cause.

Person	The e-mail contents	The embarrassment
A parent		
Your boss		
Boyfriend / girlfriend		
Your best friend		
A colleague		
Your professor		

NOTES:

Write On!

Free write for 10 minutes about alcohol. Be creative! What do television, movies and music say about using alcohol? What does traditional culture and pop culture tell us? What are your habits?

✐ Phrasal Verbs	
To get drunk	**To have a crush on**
• I want to get drunk.	• I have a crush on _____.
• I don't like to get drunk.	• He / she has a crush on _____.
• I got drunk.	• I had a crush on _____.

The Whole Story

Read these fascinating facts related to alcohol.

- The alcohol in drinks of either low alcohol content, below 15%, or high alcohol content, over 30%, tend to be absorbed into the body more slowly.
- Anyone under the age of 21 who takes out household trash containing even a single empty alcohol beverage container can be charged with illegal possession of alcohol in Missouri, USA.
- Vikings used the skulls of their enemies as drinking vessels.
- The word "toast," meaning a wish of good health, started in ancient Rome, where a piece of toasted bread was dropped into wine.

Myth

The US has very *lenient* underage drinking laws.

Fact

The US has the *strictest* youth drinking laws in the Western world, including the highest minimum drinking age in the entire world.

Myth

People in the US are generally heavy consumers of alcohol.

Fact

The US isn't even among the top ten alcohol consuming countries. It is 32nd on the list.

Top 10 Alcohol Consuming Countries

① Portugal
② Luxembourg
③ France
④ Hungary
⑤ Spain
⑥ Czech Republic
⑦ Denmark
⑧ Germany
⑨ Austria
⑩ Switzerland

NOTES:

Unit 5

The Hazards of Life

Get Real!
Discussion and Debate
for English Language Learners

Unit 05

The Hazards of Life

⏻ Themes and Topics

- Environment
- Pollution
- City life
- Health and wellness
- Children's safety
- Traffic
- Alternative solutions

🗁 Vocabulary Preview

Pollution	Danger	Conclusion	Traffic
Fumes	Significant	Weak/weakened	Deficit
Doubling	Healthily	Release	Suffer
Busy	Highway	Irritant	Disease
Asthma	Mass transportation		Solution
Alternative			

Pollution Near Homes Affects Lungs

Road pollution is a serious danger to children's health. That's the worrying conclusion of the longest and largest study ever undertaken into the effects of traffic fumes on child development.

Researchers from the University of Southern California spent 13 years studying children who lived within 500 meters of busy highways. They found that most of the 3,600 children in the study had significantly weakened lungs. Researchers said this meant the children could have breathing problems for the rest of their lives. The main author of the study W. James Gauderman said: "Someone suffering a pollution-related deficit in lung function as a child will probably have less than healthy lungs all of his or her life." He added: "If you live in a high-pollution area and live near a busy road, you get a doubling of the damage."

Gauderman and his team conducted their research on youngsters who lived near busy roads. Once a year, the team measured the children's lungpower. It checked how much air the children could release in one breath and how quickly it could be released. The team found that by their 18th birthday, children who lived within 500 meters of a highway exhaled 33 percent less air compared with children who lived one-and-a-half kilometers away. Further, the highway children's lungpower was seven percent weaker in the rate at which they could exhale. Gauderman said that: "Even if you are in a relatively low regional pollution area, living near a road produces lung problems." About a third of the children moved away from busy roads during the study but stayed near the same community. Their lungs developed more healthily.

Discussion and Debate

1. Answer the following questions related to the article.

1) What are the major problems with pollution?

   a What about air pollution?
   b What about water pollution?
   c What about noise pollution?
   d Other types?

2) Is road pollution a big problem in your community?

   a Does heavy traffic flow through your neighborhood?
   b How much time a day do you spend around road pollution?

3) What can you do as an individual to help combat pollution?

   a Have you considered recycling?
   b Have you considered becoming a volunteer?
   c Have you considered reusing products or packaging?
   d Have you thought of refusing to consume?
   e Have you thought of reducing consumption?

4) What should governments do to help solve this problem?

   a Will more regulations help the pollution problem?
   b Will big fines and fees for pollution help?
   c Will tax incentives for NOT driving help?

5) How can mass transportation be used to create alternative solutions?

  a What about extending subway lines?
  b What about extending subway hours of operation?
  c What about 24-hour bus service?
  d What about green taxis and buses?
  e What about carpool incentives?

6) How does road pollution affect children?

  a Do youngsters understand the affects pollution has on them?
  b How serious should environmental education be for children?

7) When / if you have children, where do you want to live?

  a Near the city?
  b Near the country?
  c High population density area?
  d Low population density area?
  e Why?

8) Is education the answer to the pollution problem?

  a What about formal education in schools?
  b What about education in the home?
  c What about a government campaign?
  d What about a non-governmental organization (NGO)?

9) What do you fear will happen if no action is taken?

  a Total climate change?
  b Massive extinction of plant and animal life?
  c Increase in cancer and other diseases?
  d Nothing?
  e Does it matter?

Building Vocabulary

1. Review this list of vocabulary words. Translate the English words into Korean.

▸ English	▸▸ Korean	▸ English	▸▸ Korean
Pollution		Release	
Danger		Suffer	
Conclusion		Busy	
Traffic		Highway	
Fumes		Irritant	
Significant		Disease	
Weak/weakened		Asthma	
Deficit		Mass transportation	
Doubling		Solution	
Healthily		Alternative	

2. Use the following words from part 1 in a sentence.

1) Deficit:

2) Fumes:

3) Traffic:

4) Highway:

5) Solution:

3. Find the vocabulary words located in the puzzle below.

Alternative	Asthma	Busy	Conclusion	Danger
Deficit	Disease	Doubling	Fumes	Healthily
Highway	Irritant	Mass	Pollution	Release
Significant	Solution	Suffer	Weak	Transportation

Pollution														
E	F	E	V	D	F	Y	S	G	X	G	R	L	T	A
S	V	N	S	U	O	O	S	Z	Y	M	F	R	N	S
S	X	I	M	A	L	U	E	U	I	C	A	D	O	T
A	U	E	T	U	E	S	B	N	B	N	Y	X	I	H
M	S	F	T	A	A	L	O	L	S	E	A	D	S	M
M	T	I	F	E	N	I	E	P	I	I	W	X	U	A
Y	O	Q	S	E	T	R	O	R	F	N	H	W	L	K
N	D	I	D	U	R	R	E	Y	Z	J	G	X	C	I
M	D	B	L	H	T	R	W	T	Z	K	I	Y	N	R
K	N	L	K	A	E	W	R	Z	L	E	H	X	O	R
P	O	G	T	I	C	I	F	E	D	A	K	C	C	I
P	Q	I	T	N	A	C	I	F	I	N	G	I	S	T
N	O	X	H	E	A	L	T	H	I	L	Y	F	V	A
N	D	A	N	G	E	R	O	W	C	U	V	Z	O	N
R	U	L	F	R	Y	H	S	S	J	A	C	X	Q	T

Practice Makes Perfect

1. Read the following statements about the article. Answer true or false.

a) A study into pollution and children's lungs was the largest ever. T / F

b) Researchers monitored different children for 30 years. T / F

c) The survey found almost half of children studied had lung damage. T / F

d) Living near a busy road doubles the chances of lung damage. T / F

e) Researchers tested the children's lungs on a monthly basis. T / F

f) Kids living 500 meters from busy roads had 30% less lung power. T / F

g) Living near a road is still bad even if it's in a low pollution area. T / F

h) Children who moved away from roads still suffered lung problems. T / F

2. Match the following words from the article with the best synonyms.

a) pollution   1) determined
b) children   2) comparatively
c) fumes   3) additionally
d) significantly   4) breath out
e) deficit   5) emissions
f) measured   6) reduction
g) exhale   7) proportion
h) further   8) considerably
i) rate   9) youngsters
j) relatively   10) smog

Write On!

Free write for 10 minutes about global warming and climate change. Be creative! What words come to mind when you think of the environment? What concerns do you have?

_____

_____

_____

_____

_____

_____

_____

_____

_____

_____

_____

_____

_____

_____

NOTES:

_____

_____

_____

_____

```
┌─────────────────────────────────┐
│  The Whole Story    NEWS ►       │
└─────────────────────────────────┘
```

Read these fascinating facts related to global pollution.

1. During winter months, 49 percent of soot and other particle pollution in Sacramento is caused by burning wood in fireplaces and wood stoves.

2. According to the World Health Organization, if you are one of the 18 million residents of Cairo, Egypt:
   - Breathing daily air pollution is like smoking 20 cigarettes a day
   - You take in over 20 times the acceptable level of air pollution each day

3. The risk of cancer from breathing diesel exhaust is about ten times more than ingesting all other toxic air pollutants combined, with diesel emissions contributing to over 70% of the cancer risk from air pollution in the USA. – *reported by Environmental Defense*

4. The Boston area ranks number 5 in the country for premature deaths due to diesel pollution annually. – *reported by the Clean Air Task Force*

5. According to Carnegie Institution's Department of Global Ecology, carbon dioxide (a greenhouse gas) is rising at an alarming rate. During the 1990s, carbon dioxide emissions increased approximately 1.3% each year. But since 2000, the rate has increased to 3.3% per year, with an estimated annual global CO_2 emissions increase of 35% from 1990 to 2006.

6. A recent study from Toronto Public Health estimates over 440 deaths a year in the Canadian city can be directly attributed to traffic emissions.

7. Emissions from ocean-going ships contribute to approximately 60,000 deaths each year, mostly from heart and lung-related cancers. Shanghai, Singapore and Hong Kong rank within the world's top 5 busiest ports, and experience a higher impact from emissions-related health issues.

Unit
6

Risky Fizz

Get Real!
Discussion and Debate
for English Language Learners

Unit 06

Risky Fizz

Themes and Topics

- Health
- Wellness
- Nutrition
- Obesity
- Diet
- Weight loss

Vocabulary Preview

Warnings	Press release	Labeled	Carbonated
Drowning	Worthless	Contribute	Obesity
Dental	Epidemic	Evidence	Overweight
Serving (noun)	Soft drink	Soda	Manufacturers
Appropriate	Study (noun)	Default	
High fructose corn syrup			

Soda Should Carry Warnings

Soft drinks that are full of sugar may soon have health warnings like those on cigarette packets. The Center for Science in the Public Interest (CSPI) has issued a press release calling for all sodas to be labeled.

It warns carbonated beverages are an increasing danger to our health. CSPI director Michael Jacobson stated that: "Americans are drowning in soda pop" He described soda as a "worthless" product. Carbonated soda pop provides more added sugar in a typical 2-year-old toddler's diet than cookies, candies and ice cream combined. This early start on liquid sugar creates terrible habits in teens and, eventually, adults. Extra sugar and calories found in soda contribute to obesity at every age.

Jacobson also stressed that obesity is an epidemic. Reporting in The Lancet, a British medical journal, a team of Harvard researchers presented the first evidence linking soft drink consumption to childhood obesity. They found that 12-year-olds who drank soft drinks regularly were more likely to be overweight than those who didn't.

For each additional daily serving of sugar-sweetened soft drink consumed during the nearly two-year study, the risk of obesity increased 1.6 times.

Teenagers drink an average of three cans of soda a day. This is 15 percent of their necessary calorie intake. Mr. Jacobson asked: "How did a mix of high-fructose corn syrup, water, and artificial flavors come to be the default beverage?"

He urged soft drink manufacturers to warn kids that soda results in obesity, dental problems and weak bones. He also said soda is "not appropriate for children."

Discussion and Debate

1. Answer the following questions related to the article.

   1) Do you agree with the article?

      a Should soda carry warnings?

      b Is soda truly dangerous?

      c What steps should be taken to inform the public about the dangers of soda?

   2) Should children drink soda?

      a Do the risks outweigh the benefits?

      b What are the risks of drinking soda?

      c What are the benefits?

   3) Do you drink soda?

      a Which flavor or brand do you prefer?

      b How often do you drink soda?

      c Why do you enjoy it?

   4) What does traditional cola taste like?

      a Does it have flavor?

      b Does it taste natural?

      c Does it taste chemical?

5) What other food or beverage products do you think contribute to obesity?

   a What about fast food?

   b What about coffee beverages?

   c What about alcoholic beverages?

6) Do you think your country has a problem with obesity?

   a Why or why not?

   b Are children or adults fatter in your country?

   c What does this tell you about diet and exercise?

7) Is cola a popular beverage in your country?

   a Do people drink more cola than water?

   b When do people choose cola over water or juice?

8) Should the government regulate the sale of cola?

   a What about to children?

   b What about to schools?

   c What about to academies or hagwons?

9) What do you think of parents that allow children to drink cola?

   a Do you think it does or doesn't matter?

   b Do you think they are bad parents?

   c Do you think that they are responsible if their children are obese or overweight?

10) Should children be allowed free-reign at vending machines after school or between academy lessons?

  a How does eating out of a vending machine all day affect people, including children?

  b Can children, or adults, develop soda or coffee addictions?

  c How could someone become addicted to cola?

  d Why would someone become addicted to cola?

NOTES:

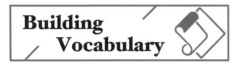
Building Vocabulary

1. Review this list of vocabulary words. Translate the English words into Korean.

▸ English	▸▸ Korean	▸ English	▸▸ Korean
Warnings		Evidence	
Press release		Overweight	
Labeled		Serving (noun)	
Carbonated		Soft drink	
Drowning		Soda	
Worthless		Manufacturers	
Contribute		Appropriate	
Obesity		Study (noun)	
Dental		Default	
Epidemic		High fructose corn syrup	

2. Which words from part 1 match the following synonyms?

1) Extremely overweight:

2) Useless:

3) Carbonated drink:

4) Outbreak:

5) Caution:

3. Seek the words. Find the vocabulary words from the box below in the puzzle.

Warnings	Press	Release	Labeled	Carbonated
Drowning	Worthless	Contribute	Obesity	Dental
Epidemic	Evidence	Overweight	Serving	Soft
Drink	Soda	Manufacturers	Appropriate	Study
Default	Fructose	Corn	Syrup	

The Dangers of Soda														
X	F	C	Q	H	W	U	Q	G	E	O	O	S	T	C
C	A	R	B	O	N	A	T	E	D	G	V	V	L	I
W	O	Y	H	S	U	O	D	W	X	S	E	L	U	M
G	J	N	Y	N	B	V	O	O	E	R	R	A	A	E
A	N	R	T	E	O	R	P	C	S	E	W	B	F	D
D	U	I	S	R	T	R	N	U	T	R	E	E	E	I
P	R	I	N	H	I	E	E	A	N	U	I	L	D	P
D	T	I	L	W	D	B	I	L	H	T	G	E	X	E
Y	X	E	N	I	O	R	U	G	E	C	H	D	Q	S
Y	S	J	V	K	P	R	I	T	F	A	T	W	L	T
S	A	E	B	O	P	H	D	M	E	F	S	A	F	U
U	T	F	R	U	C	T	O	S	E	U	T	E	E	D
U	Z	P	R	E	S	S	G	N	I	N	R	A	W	Y
M	P	G	N	I	V	R	E	S	E	A	T	F	O	S
A	H	O	T	L	X	T	L	D	S	M	C	O	R	N

Practice Makes Perfect

1. Read the following statements about the article. Answer true or false.

    a)   A new product called "liquid candy" is for sale.   T / F

    b)   A health group wants sodas to be labeled with health T / F
        warnings.

    c)   Some Americans drown in soda every year.   T / F

    d)   Obesity is an epidemic.   T / F

    e)   Early soda drinking habits ward off cancer.   T / F

    f)   Three sodas a day are 50% of a child's required daily T / F
        calories.

    g)   Drinking too much soda leads to weak bones.   T / F

    h)   The health advisory group says soda is appropriate for kids T / F
        but unhealthy for adults.

2. Fill in the following blanks with words from the article.

    _____ drinks that are full of sugar may soon have health warnings like those on cigarette packets. The Center for Science in the Public Interest (CSPI) has issued a press release calling for all sodas to be labeled. It warns carbonated beverages are an increasing _____ to our health. CSPI director Michael Jacobson stated that: "Americans are drowning in soda pop." He described soda as a "_____" product. He also stressed "obesity is an epidemic."

    The title of the press release describes soda as "liquid candy." It reports that teenagers _____ an average of three cans of soda a day. This is 15 per cent of their necessary calorie intake. Mr. Jacobson asked: "How did a solution of high-fructose corn syrup, water, and artificial flavors come to be the default beverage?" He urged soft drink manufacturers to warn kids that soda ____ obesity, dental problems and weak bones. He also said soda is "not ____ for children."

3. Decide if you agree or disagree with the following statements.

a) Soda should be banned worldwide.

b) People know that soda isn't healthy. If they drink it, that's their choice.

c) Drink manufacturers target kids - that's wrong.

d) Kids who drink too much soda have bad parents.

e) The crazy thing is that many schools serve soda with school lunches.

f) Soda consumption presents a common problem. Anything in moderation is OK.

g) People who become obese from drinking soda should sue the soda companies.

NOTES:

Free write for 10 minutes about obesity. Be creative! What words do you think of when you think of obesity? What concerns do you have about being overweight or obese? How is diet and exercise related to obesity?

🖉 Phrasal Verbs

To run into

- I ran into my teacher.
- Don't run into him.
- I run into him all of the time.

The Whole Story

Read these fascinating facts related to soda.

These are just a few of the slogans for Coca-Cola:

1893	The ideal brain tonic	1957	Have Fun! Have a Coke
1904	Coca-Cola satisfies	1960	Cool off with Coke
1938	Any time is the right time to pause and refresh	1964	You'll go better refreshed
1941	Completely refreshing	1966	Christmas without Coca-Cola- Bah, humbug!
1945	Coke means Coca-Cola	1970	Coke adds life to everything nice
1950	Time out for Coke	1979	Have a Coke and a smile
1955	Taste Treat	1980	Coke is it

Coca-Cola Fact 1: When launched, its two key ingredients were cocaine and caffeine. The cocaine was derived from the coca leaf and the caffeine from kola nut, leading to the name Coca-Cola the "K" in Kola was replaced with a "C" for marketing purposes.

Coca-Cola Fact 2: The first recipe was invented in a drugstore in Columbus, Georgia in 1885 by John Pemberton. He called it "Pemberton's French Wine Coca."

Coca-Cola Fact 3: Coca-Cola contains 34 mg of caffeine per 12 fluid ounces.

Unit
7

What a Laugh

Unit
07

What a Laugh

⏻ **Themes and Topics**

- Gender
- Humor
- Social settings
- Social coping mechanisms
- Human relationships
- Jokes

📂 **Vocabulary Preview**

Naturally	Conduct	Unicycle	Jokes
Nasty	Tease	Absolutely	Remarkable
Consistent	Aggression	In-laws	Automatically
Lulls	Conversation	Claim	Observe
Comedy	Mock	Tend	Comedy

Men Have More Laughs

Men are naturally funnier than women. This is the claim of a UK male professor, Sam Shuster. He conducted research on 400 different people as he rode his unicycle around his town. He observed the reaction of onlookers and discovered that men made more jokes about him than women, and that men's jokes were more aggressive. He said three-quarters of male "jokers" mocked him and made nasty comments, while most women tended to tease him with a smile. He said: "The difference between the men and women was absolutely remarkable and consistent."

Professor Shuster believes the male hormone testosterone is the cause of men being funnier. He found that teenage boys were aggressive in their humor and this aggression changed with older men into a funnier form of joking.

Earlier research suggests women and men use humor differently. One study said women tend to tell fewer jokes than men and male comedians outnumber female ones. Another showed men look more for a punch line. Men also use people they know as the subject of their jokes, often in a negative way. Married men seem to like hearing and making jokes about mothers-in-law.

British comedian John Moloney disagreed with Professor Shuster's findings. He said that in his 21-year career in comedy, he had never noticed that men were funnier than women. He stated: "The difference is that if a group of women were together and the conversation lulls, they don't automatically start telling jokes, which men do. It then becomes a bit of a competition, but that doesn't mean to say men are funnier."

Discussion and Debate

1. Answer the following questions related to the article.

1) Do you agree with the article? Are men funnier than women?

    a Why or why not?
    b Do you think you're funny?
    c Why or why not?

2) In your group of friends, are the men or women funnier?

    a Who tells jokes more often?
    b What is the nature of the jokes?

3) Does a sense of humor change from culture to culture?

    a How is British humor different from Korean humor?
    b What about American humor?
    c What about Japanese humor?

4) Do men and women tell different kinds of jokes?

    a Whose jokes are wittier?
    b Whose jokes are dirtier?

5) Do you like to laugh?

    a Why or why not?
    b How often do you laugh in a day?
    c How do you feel when you laugh?

6) Does laughing change your emotional state?

a Does it make you feel happy when you are sad?

b Does it increase your happiness?

c Do you cry when you laugh?

7) Are all jokes funny? What about these:

a Jokes about family members

b Jokes about the opposite sex

c Jokes about current events

d Jokes about sex

8) Why do some people laugh when other people don't?

a Is it culture?

b Is it language?

c Is it family environment?

9) What is the relationship between humor and television?

a Do television programs encourage certain types of humor?

b Is this a positive or negative trend?

c Why?

10) Can a person learn to become funny?

a Is being funny genetic?

b Is it related to IQ?

c Is it related to EQ?

d Is it related to social status?

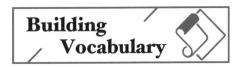

1. Review this list of vocabulary words. Translate the English words into Korean.

▶ English	▶▶ Korean	▶ English	▶▶ Korean
Naturally		In-laws	
Conduct		Automatically	
Unicycle		Lulls	
Jokes		Conversation	
Nasty		Claim	
Tease		Observe	
Absolutely		Comedy	
Remarkable		Mock	
Consistent		Tend	
Aggression		Comedy	

2. Use the following words from part 1 in a sentence.

1) Tend:

2) Tease:

3) Lulls:

4) Aggression:

5) Comedy:

Practice Makes Perfect

1. Read the following statements about the article. Answer true or false.

   a) A scientist has discovered men have funnier faces than   T / F
       women.

   b) The scientist conducted his research while riding a unicycle.   T / F

   c) The scientist believes male hormones make men funnier.   T / F

   d) He said men become funnier as they get older.   T / F

   e) Research shows there are more male than female comedians. T / F

   f) Studies suggest men are more interested in a joke's punch   T / F
       line.

   g) Men dislike hearing jokes about their wife's mother.   T / F

   h) Men seem to be more competitive than women at joke   T / F
       telling.

2. Fill in the following words or phrases with the word or words from the article.

   Men are naturally funnier than women. This is the _____ of a UK
   male professor, Sam Shuster. He _____ research on 400 different people
   as he unicycled around his town. He observed the reaction of _____ and
   discovered that men made more jokes about him than women, and that men's
   jokes were more aggressive. He said three-quarters of male "jokers" _____
   him and made nasty _____, while most women tended to tease him with
   a _____. He said: "The difference between the men and women was
   absolutely _____ and consistent." Professor Shuster believes the male

hormone testosterone is the cause of men being funnier. He found that teenage boys were aggressive in their humor and this aggression changed with older men into a funnier _____ of joking.

3. With a partner, discuss whether men or women are better at the following activities:

• cooking	• reading a map
• cleaning	• apologizing
• driving	• throwing a party
• dancing	• telling a lie

NOTES:

Write On!

Free write for 10 minutes about humor and jokes. Be creative! What is funny to you? What kind of jokes and humor do you like? Does humor vary from culture to culture?

✎ Phrasal Verbs

To make fun of

- I made fun of him.
- I don't like to be made fun of.
- Make fun of it!

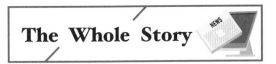

The Whole Story

Read these fascinating facts related to laughter.

Punctuation Effect

One of the key features of natural laughter is its **placement in speech**, linguists say. Laughter almost always occurs during pauses at the end of phrases.

This strong relationship between laughter and speech is much like punctuation in written communication – that's why it's called the **punctuation effect!**

Laughter is Contagious

Many researchers believe that the purpose of laughter is related to **making and strengthening human connections**.

Laughter occurs when people are **comfortable** with one another, when they feel **open** and **free**. And the more laughter there is, the more bonding occurs within the group.

The feedback "loop" of bonding-laughter-more bonding, combined with the common desire not to be singled out from the group, may be another reason why laughter is often contagious.

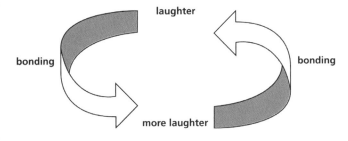

Unit
8

The Truth as Authority

Get Real!
Discussion and Debate
for English Language Learners

Unit 08

The Truth as Authority

⏻ **Themes and Topics**

- Terrorism
- Conspiracy theories
- US politics

📂 **Vocabulary Preview**

Conspiracy	Consensus	Regarding	Sufficiently
Impending	Intentionally	Suspected	Motives
Pretext	Justify	Facilitate	Restrict
Civil liberties	Demolition	Accuracy	Mainstream
Arguably	Compelling	Criticism	Deceit

Conspiracy Theories and 9/11

On September 11, 2001 the world watched the news in shock as two planes hit two buildings, and three buildings fell. Since then, many reports, theories and conspiracies have been proposed in order to explain the events of that day and the years to come.

Conspiracy theories are ideas that reject the official consensus regarding the September 11 attacks in the United States. These theories assert that the official report on the events is not sufficiently direct, thorough or truthful.

Conspiracy theories are not new, rather they have always accompanied mainstream ideas and theories. The deaths of US President John F. Kennedy, Princess Diana, and Marilyn Monroe have all been subject to many conspiracy theories.

The 9/11 Truth Movement, is the name adopted by organizations and individuals who question the mainstream account of the attacks. Generally, individuals and groups belonging to the 9/11 Truth Movement reject the accuracy of the mainstream account of the attacks, demand a new investigation into the attacks, and often investigate aspects of the September 11 attacks themselves. A prominent claim is that the collapse of the World Trade Center was the result of a controlled demolition.

By 2004, conspiracy theories about the September 11 attacks began to gain ground in the United States because of the growing criticism of the Iraq War and the presidency of George W. Bush, who had been reelected that year. This movement is still strong, even after the election of President Barak Obama, who was inaugurated in 2009.

Conspiracy theories, whether they are about 9/11, or the deaths of actors or actresses, open people up to the possibility that as a society, we might not have the correct answers to very important questions. The truth is always waiting to be told and everyone seems to have a different version. Americans may not yet know what happened on 9/11, but with each fact they learn, the world comes closer to knowing why, when two planes hit two buildings, three buildings fell down.

NOTES:

Discussion and Debate

1. Answer the following questions related to the article.

1) Do you believe the mainstream theories about the 9/11 attacks on the United States?

   a Why or why not?
   b Why would anyone want to cover-up the truth?
   c Who is to blame for a cover-up, if there is one?

2) Why did the World Trade Center buildings fall?

   a Because airplanes hit them?
   b Because of a controlled demolition?
   c Because people needed to die to go to war in Iraq?
   d Because of something else?

3) Who is responsible for the attacks of 9/11:

   a Osama Bin Laden and Al-Qaeda?
   b George W. Bush?
   c The United States government?
   d The hijackers on the flights?

4) Do you know of any other conspiracies?

   a What about the Apollo moon landing?
   b What about the death of President John F. Kennedy?
   c What about the use of fluoride in water?

d What about the death of Princess Diana?

e Are there any conspiracy theories in your country?

5) Does the War on Terror really exist?

a What or who is this terror we are at war with?

b What is happening to support the terror?

c What is happening to stop the terror?

d Are you scared of a terrorist attack in your own country?

6) Do you think President Barack Obama will change anything about the War on Terror?

a Why or why not?

b What about US troops in the Middle East?

c What about inflated military spending?

7) Is the Axis of Evil related to the War on Terror?

a What about North Korea?

b What about US troops in South Korea?

c What about a country's right to defend itself?

d What about the idea of autonomy?

8) Does Al-Qaeda have the right to arm and defend it cause?

a Why or why not?

b Who decides that a group can or cannot have weapons?

c Who decides if a group is bad or good?

9) Does North Korea have the right to defend itself?

> a Is it a real country?
> b Does it pose a real threat to the South?
> c Should they be allowed to develop nuclear weapons?
> d Who decides these things?

10) Will you do more research on 9/11 and possible conspiracy theories?

> a Why or why not?
> b What information will you look for?
> c What questions do you have about the events?
> d Do you believe what the governments tell people, just because the information is coming from the government?

NOTES:

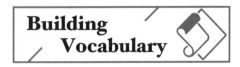

Building
Vocabulary

1. Review this list of vocabulary words. Translate the English words into Korean.

▸ English	▸▸ Korean	▸ English	▸▸ Korean
Conspiracy		Facilitate	
Consensus		Restrict	
Regarding		Civil liberties	
Sufficiently		Demolition	
Impending		Accuracy	
Intentionally		Mainstream	
Suspected		Arguably	
Motives		Compelling	
Pretext		Criticism	
Justify		Deceit	

2. Match the following synonyms with vocabulary words from part 1.

1) Assumed:

2) Normal:

3) Excuse:

4) Agreement:

5) Lies:

Practice Makes Perfect

1. Read the following statements about the article. Answer true or false.

a) Conspiracy theories are mainstream ideas. T / F

b) The events from 9/11 are still in debate. T / F

c) The 9/11 Truth Movement wants a new investigation into the events of the day. T / F

d) Some people think that President Bush used 9/11 to go to war with China. T / F

e) One theory is that the 9/11 attacks fueled military spending and suspended civil liberties. T / F

f) American people know the truth about what happened on 9/11. T / F

g) American people supported President Bush 100% of the time. T / F

h) A popular claim is that the collapse of the buildings was because of controlled demolition. T / F

2. Fill in the following blanks with words or phrases from the article.

9/11 _____ theories are ideas that reject the official _____ regarding the September 11 _____ in the United States. These theories _____ that the official report on the events is not _____ direct, thorough or truthful. Many critics claim that individuals in the government of the United States knew of the _____ attacks and _____ failed to act on that knowledge. Some critics state that the attacks could have been a _____ _____ _____ carried out by a private network of

high-level officials in the U.S. Government. The common suspected
_____ were the use of the attacks as a pretext to justify overseas
wars, to facilitate increased military spending, and to restrict domestic
_____   _____.

3. Rate the following threats from 1-8, 1 being the most important and 8 being the least important. What do you think is the most important threat today?

_____ Finding Osama Bin Laden   _____ International weapons trade
_____ North Korea and nuclear weapons   _____ Plane and flight safety
_____ Ddok-do and Japan   _____ School shootings
_____ The international drug trade   _____ Internet security

NOTES:

Write On!

Free write for 10 minutes about 9/11. Be creative! What do you think happened? Why? What was the purpose of the event? How do you feel about it today? Where were you when you heard about the attacks?

> ✎ Phrasal Verbs
>
> To look up
>
> - I want to look up the number.
> - I want to look the number up.
> - Look it up!
> - He looked it up.

The Whole Story

Read these fascinating facts about the timeline of the 9/11 terrorist attacks.

September 11, 2001—Timeline for the Day of the Attacks

8:20 AM: Air traffic controllers suspect Flight 11 has been hijacked. [NY Times, 9/15/01]

8:40 AM: NORAD is notified of hijacking. [NY Times, 10/16/01, 8:38 AM Washington Post, 9/15/01]

8:46 AM: Flight 11 crashes into the WTC (World Trade Center) north tower. [**approximately** *26 minutes after controllers lost contact*] [New York Times, 9/12/01]

8:46 AM: President Bush later states, "I was sitting outside the classroom and I saw an airplane hit the tower. The TV was on." [CNN, 12/4/01] "When we walked into the classroom, I had seen this plane fly into the first building." [White House, 1/5/02] *There was no live coverage of the first crash on TV and President Bush was in a classroom reading with children at the time of the second crash.*

8:52 AM: Two F-15s take off from Otis Air Force Base. [Washington Post, 9/15/01] They go after Flight 175. Major General Paul Weaver, director of the Air National Guard, states "the pilots flew like a scalded ape, topping 500 mph but were unable to catch up to the airliner. We had a nine-minute window, and in excess of 100 miles to intercept 175," he said. "There was just literally no way." [Dallas Morning News, 9/15/01] F-15's fly at up to 2.5 times the speed of sound [*1875 mph or 30+ miles a minute or 270+ miles in nine minutes*] and are designed for low-altitude, high-speed, precision attacks. [BBC]

8:56 AM: By this time, it is evident that Flight 77 is lost. The FAA, already in contact with the Pentagon about the two hijackings out of Boston, reportedly doesn't notify NORAD of this until 9:24, **28 minutes later**. [*see 9:10 AM for comparison*, New York Times, 10/16/01]

9:03 AM: Flight 175 crashes into the south WTC tower. [*23 minutes after NORAD notified, 43 minutes after air traffic control lost contact with pilots*][New York Times, 9/12/01, CNN, 9/12/01]

9:10 AM: Major General Paul Weaver states Flight 77 came back on the (radar) scope at 9:10 in West Virginia. [Dallas Morning News, 9/15/01] Another report states the military was notified of Flight 77 several minutes after 9:03. [Washington Post, 9/15/01]

9:24 AM [*? – see above*]: The FAA, who 28 minutes earlier had discovered Flight 77 off course and heading east over West Virginia, reportedly notifies NORAD. A Pentagon spokesman says, "The Pentagon was simply not aware that this aircraft was coming our way." [Newsday, 9/23/01, New York Times, 10/16/01] Yet since the first crash, military officials in a Pentagon command center were urgently talking to law enforcement and air traffic control officials about what to do. [New York Times, 9/15/01]

9:28 AM: Air traffic control learns that Flight 93 has been hijacked. [MSNBC, 7/30/02]

9:38 AM: Flight 77 crashes into the Pentagon. [*42 minutes or more after contact was lost, one hour after NORAD notification of first hijacking*][New York Times, 10/16/01, 9:43 CNN, 9/12/01]

9:59 AM: The south tower of the World Trade Center collapses. [New York Times, 9/12/01]

10:10 AM: Flight 93 crashes in Pennsylvania. [*42 minutes after contact was lost, 90 minutes after NORAD notification of first hijacking. What happened to sophisticated military radar systems and jet fighter scramble procedures?*][CNN, 9/12/02]

10:28 AM: The World Trade Center north tower collapses. [CNN, 9/12/01, NY Times, 9/12/01]

5:20 PM: Building 7 of the World Trade Center collapses. [CNN, 9/12/01] Though the media claims fires brought the building down, the building's owner Larry Silverstein later recounts the story of the collapse of this 47-story skyscraper in a PBS documentary *America Rebuilds*, "I remember getting a call from the fire department commander. ... I said ... maybe the smartest thing to do is to pull it. And they made that decision to pull, and then we watched the building collapse." [PBS Documentary]

Unit
9

What Not to Wear

Get Real!
Discussion and Debate
for English Language Learners

Unit 09 \ What Not to Wear

⏻ Themes and Topics

- Fashion
- Job interview
- Pop culture

📁 Vocabulary Preview

Impression	Potential	Employer	Judgment
Based	Professionally	Casual	Candidate
Scruffy	Appropriate	Attire	Dry-clean
Polish	Trimmed	Portfolio	Briefcase
Conservative	Coordinated	Neutral	Neatly

The Great Fashion Debate

Today, we live in a society of ever-increasing independence, especially when it comes to personal style. But how much of our own personal style should we express during a job interview? How fashion-forward should we be, and how truly important is what we wear?

Is the first impression you make on a potential employer is the most important one? Some say yes, and other people say no. The first judgment an interviewer makes is going to be based on how you look and what you are wearing. So, is it important to dress professionally for a job interview, even if the work environment is casual? Even if you say all of the right things, if you wear all of the wrong things, that is how you will be remembered. Interviewers judge you based upon what you wear and the style you show.

You'll want that first impression to be not just good, but great, so what should you wear? Some people think that the candidate dressed in a suit and tie is going to make a much better impression than the candidate dressed in scruffy jeans and a t-shirt. For women, young people might think that it is okay to go to an interview in trendy heels and a mini skirt, while older women choose a more conservative look. For men, tee shirts, even if they are a luxury brand, are not generally acceptable. People say: dress well and you will feel great. But what if you think you look great, and you new boss does not?

How can interview fashion go wrong? Other than style, many people forget to consider the fit of their clothing. Ill-fitting pants or a too-tight blouse are both uncomfortable and unattractive. One thing is for sure; planning ahead makes all of the difference.

Finishing touches are always important. Jewelry is an important accessory for many people, but which items do you wear, and which do you leave at home? A delicate pair of earrings for women, and a nice tie or cufflinks for men, is a popular choice. If you are not a mild person and prefer to wear bold accessories, you might wish to wear something more fitting to your character. Whatever your style, the age-old question remains; which is better, less or more?

How much perfume or cologne should you spray before an interview? Also, for women, what style of make-up is most preferable? What about bold or unusual shades of color on the lips and eyes?

However mild or wild you are, remember that the most important thing you can wear is a confident smile. An interview is about selling yourself and a smile is the best accessory anyone can wear.

NOTES:

Discussion and Debate

1. Answer the following questions related to the article.

1) Have you been on a job interview?

   a What did you wear?
   b How did you feel when you arrived to your interview?
   c Would you change anything about the way you dressed for the interview?

2) Do you agree with the interview attire recommendations from the article?

   a For men?
   b For women?
   c Would you change any of these?
   d Why or why not?

3) How long should woman's skirt be?

   a For an interview?
   b For school?
   c For a party?
   d For work?

4) How long should man's hair be?

   a For an interview?
   b For a professional job?
   c For attracting a woman?

5) What are some major fashion Don'ts?

- a Innerwear as outerwear?
- b Too-short skirts?
- c Men with too many buttons undone on a shirt?
- d Ill-fitting clothing? Too tight or too loose?
- e Excessive make-up?
- f Excessive aftershave or perfume?

6) How do you want your girlfriend or boyfriend to dress?

- a What is sexy?
- b What is conservative?
- c What is undesirable?

7) Does your fashion affect your ideas of body image?

- a If yes, is it a positive or negative change?
- b How do you feel when you are well dressed?
- c How do you feel when you are under-dressed for an occasion?
- d What else affects your idea of body image?

8) Do you follow trends?

- a What is your favorite current trend?
- b What trend are you tired of?
- c Why does something become trendy?
- d Who decides what's trendy?

9) What is the relationship between culture and fashion?

  a Can exposure to certain media outlets change how you feel about your fashion style?

  b Do celebrity fashion styles affect what you like and dislike about fashion?

  c Have you ever bought something that you didn't like because someone famous wore the item?

10) How far have you taken fashion?

  a Have you taken a fashion risk?

  b Have you worn something that your friends hated, but you loved?

  c Who is your fashion icon?

  d Who do you know that is known for being fashionable?

  e How important is fashion, really?

NOTES:

Building Vocabulary

1. Review this list of vocabulary words. Translate the English words into Korean.

▶ English	▶▶ Korean	▶ English	▶▶ Korean
Impression		Attire	
Potential		Dry-clean	
Employer		Polish	
Judgment		Trimmed	
Based		Portfolio	
Professionally		Briefcase	
Casual		Conservative	
Candidate		Coordinated	
Scruffy		Neutral	
Appropriate			

2. Match the following synonyms with vocabulary words from part 1.

1) Pale:

2) Matching:

3) Possibility:

4) Idea:

5) Clothing:

Practice Makes Perfect

1. Read the following statements about the article. Answer true or false.

   a)   Women should wear short skirts to job interviews.   T / F

   b)   Men should wear little or no jewelry.   T / F

   c)   A first impression is very important.   T / F

   d)   You should never chew gum in an interview.   T / F

   e)   Drinking coffee or soda is okay at an interview.   T / F

   f)   Perfume and aftershave is never ok, in any amount.   T / F

   g)   Show your personal style, no matter what it is.   T / F

   h)   Try on your clothing the night before to avoid any problems. T / F

2. What should you wear to the following events? Discuss them with a partner and decide what you would or would not wear.

• University class	• Date with girl/boyfriend
• Dance club	• Wedding
• Health club	• Shopping with friends
• Picnic	• Funeral

3. Seek the words. Find the vocabulary words from the box below in the puzzle.

Appropriate	Attire	Based	Briefcase	Candidate
Casual	Conservative	Coordinated	Dry-Clean	Employer
Impression	Judgment	Neatly	Neutral	Polish
Portfolio	Potential	Scruffy	Professionally	Trimmed

What to Wear														
A	H	E	O	E	R	A	S	Q	I	F	O	T	Y	N
J	P	F	T	X	M	C	T	M	C	I	I	L	D	A
U	F	P	X	A	R	P	P	T	L	U	L	C	K	E
D	D	Z	R	U	D	R	L	O	I	A	I	O	Q	L
G	P	E	F	O	E	I	F	O	N	R	I	O	S	C
M	N	F	S	S	P	T	D	O	Y	G	E	R	L	Y
E	Y	U	S	A	R	R	I	N	G	E	G	D	A	R
N	D	I	C	O	B	S	I	R	A	J	R	I	R	D
T	O	Z	P	F	S	U	V	A	G	C	S	N	T	P
N	T	Y	D	E	M	M	I	R	T	J	I	A	U	O
C	N	D	F	C	A	S	U	A	L	E	V	T	E	L
K	K	O	H	B	R	I	E	F	C	A	S	E	N	I
B	R	Z	Y	L	T	A	E	N	F	L	F	D	Z	S
P	L	A	I	T	N	E	T	O	P	D	E	N	N	H
C	O	N	S	E	R	V	A	T	I	V	E	H	O	A

4. Review the following suggestions for interview attire for men and women. Do you agree or disagree? Discuss your opinion with a partner. Discuss your opinion with the class.

Men's Interview Attire

- Suit (solid color - navy or dark grey)
- Long sleeve shirt (white or coordinated with the suit)
- Belt
- Tie
- Dark socks, conservative leather shoes
- Little or no jewelry
- Neat, professional hairstyle
- Minimum Amount of Aftershave
- Neatly trimmed nails
- Portfolio or briefcase

Women's Interview Attire

- Suit (navy, black or dark grey)
- The suit skirt should be long enough so you can sit down comfortably
- Coordinated blouse
- Conservative shoes
- Limited jewelry; no dangling earrings or arms full of bracelets
- No jewelry is better than cheap jewelry
- Professional hairstyle
- Neutral pantyhose
- Light make-up and perfume
- Neatly manicured clean nails
- Portfolio or briefcase

What Not to Bring to the Interview

- Cell phone
- Ipod or MP3 player
- Gum
- Coffee, tea or soda

Free write for 10 minutes about fashion. Be creative! What do you like to wear? What is appropriate to wear and when is it best to wear it? How do you dress to work? School? Church?

🖉 Phrasal Verbs
To go for
• The same goes for you!
• It doesn't go for us!
• It went for them, as well.

Read these fascinating facts about fashion.

1) The Function of Buttons on Jacket Sleeves

Have you ever asked yourself why there are buttons on the ends of jacket sleeves? According to information passed down through the ages, none other than Napoleon Bonaparte dictated that buttons be attached to jacket sleeves to stop the annoying habit soldiers had of wiping their runny noses on their jacket sleeves.

2) What Makes an Item Vintage?

A clothing item is considered vintage if it dates from 1920 to 1960. After that date, an item is considered to be retro, not vintage.

3) The Invention of the Bra

Would you believe the bra wasn't patented until 1914? A young New York socialite named Mary Phelps created the bra. She grew weary of having her camisole show when she wore a lace blouse. Using handkerchiefs, she designed the first rudimentary bra, which she eventually had patented in 1914. Women everywhere loved Mary's new design and the first bra took off in a big way.

4) The History of the Skirt

Did you know the skirt is the second oldest women's garment in history? Only the loincloth precedes it in age. In Egyptian times, both men and women wore the skirt. This can be verified by looking at drawings from ancient times.

Unit 10

All We Need Is Love

Get Real!
Discussion and Debate
for English Language Learners

Unit 10

All We Need Is Love

⏻ **Themes and Topics**

- Love
- Family
- Romance
- Relationships

📂 **Vocabulary Preview**

Inquire	Throughout	Unconditional	Nurturing
Maternal	Lust	Desire	Consider
Platonic	Coexist	Assure	Agape
Selfless	Potentially	Willing	Self-sacrificing
Altruistic	Complications	Monument	Pray

Love, Sweet Love

Poets, presidents, and philosophers alike have all inquired about one of the greatest mysteries known to man; love. What is love? Why do we love? How do we know what love is? And why can we love in so many different ways? If love makes the world go 'round, why is it so hard to describe?

Love begins when we are too young to remember and continues throughout our lives. As babies, we begin to show love for our parents, who feed, clothe and protect us, as we mature. This is maternal love, which is thought to be unconditional, protective and nurturing.

As young children, we love dolls and toys, swimming in the summer and eating ice cream. We love our brothers and sisters and we love others as if they were our family. This is platonic love. Platonic love can exist between men and women, two men or two women. Platonic love is nonphysical. This means that it is nonsexual. When humans feel platonic love it does not induce feelings of lust or desire. It can also be considered spiritual in nature

Romantic love is the love that brings two people together, to share a life, or a moment in time. This is the kind of love that men and women, and sometimes two men or two women, share. This love is unique because it gives people the feelings of desire, passion and lust. The desire to have sex frequently comes from romantic love. Men and women have used sex as a means of expressing romantic love for thousands of years. While love and sex are not the same thing, they can coexist together. However, romantic love does not need sex to be authentic, just as sex does not assure that love is there.

Agape love is the selfless love of others. This love is potentially the most difficult to describe as there are few examples in everyday life. Agape love is self-sacrificing and altruistic. When someone is willing to sacrifice anything and everything for the good of other people, this is agape love.

For whatever complications love brings humanity, it also brings great joy. The Taj Mahal was built as a monument to love and Shakespeare's Romeo and Juliet died for love. Although they may not understand love, human beings act out of love; they die for love, kill for love, work for love and pray for love.

NOTES:

Discussion and Debate

1. Answer the following questions related to the article.

1) Who loves you?

   a Family?
   b Friends?
   c Boyfriend or girlfriend?
   d Pets?

2) What does it mean to "believe in love?"

   a Does it mean that we are looking for love?
   b Does it mean we accept the pain associated with love?
   c Does it mean that we want to love or be loved?

3) Which love is the most important kind?

   a Maternal?
   b Platonic?
   c Romantic?
   d Agape?

4) What is the purpose of romantic love?

   a To unite men and women?
   b To create families and babies?

5) Can more than one type of love exist at the same time?

 - a What about platonic and maternal?
 - b What about romantic and platonic?
 - c What about agape and romantic?
 - d How does two types of love together make the love better?
 - e How does it make it more complicated?

6) Is romantic love between men and women the same as romantic love between two men or two women?

 - a Why or why not?
 - b Does sexual orientation matter in regards to love?
 - c Who can judge if it is the same or not?
 - d How would you know if you are not gay or lesbian?
 - e Do gay and lesbian couples have the right to express romantic love the same way as heterosexual couples?

7) What does love feel like?

 - a Soft and romantic?
 - b Cold and painful?
 - c Complicated?
 - d Natural?

8) What is the difference between loving someone and being "in love" with them?

 - a Is one deeper or more intense?
 - b Is one romantic?
 - c Are both romantic?
 - d Is one platonic or maternal?

e Who can you be "in love" with?

f Who can you love?

9) How do you know that you are in love?

a Is it a feeling?

b What does it feel like?

c How do you know that you can love someone "forever"?

10) When can people begin to feel love?

a What age?

b What maturity level?

c Are we born knowing how to love?

d Does culture teach us how and whom to love?

NOTES:

Building Vocabulary

1. Review this list of vocabulary words. Translate the English words into Korean.

▶ English	▶▶ Korean	▶ English	▶▶ Korean
Inquire		Assure	
Throughout		Agape	
Unconditional		Selfless	
Nurturing		Potentially	
Maternal		Willing	
Lust		Self-sacrificing	
Desire		Altruistic	
Consider		Complications	
Platonic		Monument	
Coexist		Pray	

2. Which words from part 1 match the following synonyms?

1) Friendly:

2) Motherly:

3) Think:

4) During:

5) Memorial:

3. Seek the words. Find the vocabulary words from the box below in the puzzle.

Inquire	Throughout	Unconditional	Nurturing	Maternal
Lust	Desire	Consider	Platonic	Coexist
Assure	Agape	Selfless	Potentially	Willing
Altruistic	Monument	Self-sacrificing	Complications	Pray

Love, Love, Love													
U	N	C	O	N	D	I	T	I	O	N	A	L	R	G
C	G	B	L	L	W	H	O	Z	T	E	M	E	N	L
U	O	N	F	Y	U	G	L	H	K	D	D	I	M	A
S	R	M	I	J	E	S	R	Q	H	I	C	M	P	N
L	E	N	P	R	Z	O	T	X	S	I	W	O	O	R
G	V	L	U	L	U	O	C	N	F	Z	I	N	T	E
M	N	S	F	G	I	T	O	I	R	N	E	U	E	T
M	S	I	H	L	S	C	R	E	Q	P	R	M	N	A
A	N	O	L	O	E	C	A	U	X	R	I	E	T	M
J	U	Q	K	L	A	S	I	T	N	A	S	N	I	C
T	A	F	G	S	I	R	S	Y	I	Y	E	T	A	M
I	T	F	F	O	E	W	N	D	A	O	D	S	L	E
C	P	L	A	T	O	N	I	C	D	H	N	O	L	M
U	E	C	I	T	S	I	U	R	T	L	A	S	Y	E
S	T	S	I	X	E	O	C	A	G	A	P	E	P	L

Practice Makes Perfect

1. Read the following statements about the article. Answer true or false.

a)	Love is the same for all people.	T / F
b)	Parents give children agape love.	T / F
c)	Maternal love comes from parents.	T / F
d)	Agape love is selfless love of other people.	T / F
e)	If you love your friend, this is called platonic love.	T / F
f)	Romantic love includes feelings of passion and desire.	T / F
g)	The Taj Mahal was built for love.	T / F

2. Decide if you agree or disagree with the following statements. Then on the lines below, write a sentence explaining why you agree or disagree.

a) Love makes the world go round.

_____

b) Love is the answer to all of life's problems.

_____

c) Love is natural.

_____

d) Husbands and wives need love to make a marriage work.

_____

e) Love is not the most important virtue in the world.

_____

f) Love hurts.

_____

NOTES:

_____

_____

_____

_____

_____

Write On!

Free write for 10 minutes about love. Be creative! What words do you think of when you think of love? Have you ever been in romantic love? Do you love your friends and family? How are these types of love different?

📝 Phrasal Verbs

To fall in love

- I fell in love.
- He fell in love with her.
- I want to fall in love.

The Whole Story

Read these fascinating facts related to love.

1) Men who kiss their wives in the morning live five years longer than those who don't.

2) People are more likely to tilt their heads to the right when kissing instead of the left. Sixty five percent of people go to the right!

3) Feminist women are more likely than other females to be in a romantic relationship.

4) Two-thirds of people report that they fall in love with someone they've known for some time vs. someone that they just met.

5) The women of the Tiwi tribe in the South Pacific are married at birth.

6) Eleven percent of women have gone online and done research on a person they were dating or were about to meet, versus seven percent of men.

7) Couples' personalities converge over time to make partners more and more similar.

8) The oldest known love song was written 4,000 years ago and comes from an area between the Tigris and Euphrates Rivers.

9) Forty-three percent of women prefer their partners never sign "love" to a card unless they are ready for commitment.

10) People who are newly in love produce decreased levels of the hormone serotonin – as low as levels seen in people with obsessive-compulsive disorder. Perhaps that's why it's so easy to feel obsessed when you're smitten.

11) Every Valentine's Day, Verona, the Italian city where Shakespeare's play Romeo and Juliet took place, receives around 1,000 letters addressed to Juliet.

12) When we get dumped, for a period of time we love the person who rejected us even more, says Dr. Helen Fisher of Rutgers University and author of Why We Love. The brain regions that lit up when we were in a happy union continue to be active.

13) One in five long-term love relationships began with one or both partners being involved with others.

NOTES:

Unit 11

The Taliban Today

Get Real!
Discussion and Debate
for English Language Learners

Unit 11

The Taliban Today

⏻ **Themes and Topics**

- Pakistan
- Politics
- Development
- Security
- Social unrest

📂 **Vocabulary Preview**

Humanitarian	Crisis	Unfolding	Forces
Escape	Fundamentalist	Alliance	Regroup
Internal	Refugees	Curfew	Partition
Rebel	Offensive	Heavily-armed	Militants
Casualty	Convoy	Overloaded	Civilians
Insurgents			

Pakistan Fighting Forces 2 Million to Flee

A new humanitarian crisis is unfolding in Pakistan. Hundreds of thousands of Pakistanis have fled their homes to escape fighting between the Pakistan Army and Taliban forces.

The Taliban is an Islamic fundamentalist political movement that governed Afghanistan from 1996 until 2001, when its leaders were removed from power by Northern Alliance and NATO forces. It has regrouped and since 2004 revived as a strong insurgency movement.

There are estimates that nearly one-and-a-half million people in the Swat Valley area of Pakistan are displaced. The United Nations says that 2 million civilians moved to avoid the violence.

Huge numbers of internal refugees were on the move as the army eased a curfew. Hundreds of cars and overloaded buses formed a huge convoy. They were all heading for refugee camps in the south. Pakistan's Prime Minister, Yousuf Raza Gilani said the growing refugee crisis was his nation's worst after the partition of India and Pakistan in 1947.

Fighting between the Pakistan military and Taliban rebels has got worse in recent days. Army commanders are increasing their efforts to root out the militants. Pakistan's 'Dawn' newspaper reported heavy fighting in the northwest of the country as the military went on the offensive. Army Major General Athar Abbas said his troops killed at least 55 Taliban fighters in recent attacks.

More than 15,000 Pakistan troops have moved into the Swat Valley to take on around 5,000 heavily armed militants. A Taliban spokesman denied the casualty figures. Muslim Khan said his fighters have killed over 37 Pakistani soldiers in fighting since Wednesday. He said Pakistani troops killed just three Taliban soldiers.

Discussion and Debate

1. Answer the following questions related to the article.

1) Whose responsibility is the Pakistan crisis?

   a Is it Taliban's fault?

   b Is it Pakistan government's fault?

   c Is it the fault of citizens?

2) Where should the 2 million Pakistani people go?

   a Nowhere?

   b To different countries, relocated by the UN?

   c Home?

   d Jail?

3) If you were fleeing your home, what would you take?

   a Clothing

   b Family pictures?

   c Pets?

   d Weapons?

   e Food?

   f Religious items?

4) What is war?

   a Is the Pakistani crisis a war?

   b What are the characteristics of a war?

5) Is war bad?

  a What about defending your land?

  b What about defending your life?

  c What about defending your family and loved ones?

  d What about defending your country?

6) When is it okay to kill another person?

  a Is war an excuse to kill?

  b Who is responsible for the deaths of war?

  c Should we help people that lose family to war?

7) Will the world always have refugee camps?

  a Why do we need them?

  b What purpose do they serve?

  c What pushes people to leave their home to live in refugee camps?

8) What other humanitarian problems exist today?

  a What about HIV and AIDS?

  b What about nuclear weapons?

  c What about North Korea?

  d Is poverty a problem?

  e Is hunger a problem?

  f Are child soldiers a problem?

9) What do you think governments that allow their citizens to suffer?

  a Should they be forced out of office?

  b Should the UN stop them?

  c Should the world support them?

  d Is it the choice of each country how they wish to be governed?

10) What is the cause of war?

> a Is it selfishness or greed?
>
> b Is it the need to protect what we have?
>
> c Is it the desire to protect what we have?
>
> d Is it natural?
>
> e Is it a part of "God's Will?"
>
> f Is it possible to live without war and dispute?

NOTES:

Building Vocabulary

1. Review this list of vocabulary words. Translate the English words into Korean.

▸ English	▸▸ Korean	▸ English	▸▸ Korean
Humanitarian		Curfew	
Crisis		Partition	
Unfolding		Rebel	
Forces		Offensive	
Escape		Heavily-armed	
Fundamentalist		Militants	
Alliance		Casualty	
Regroup		Convoy	
Internal		Overloaded	
Refugee		Civilians	

2. Which words from part 1 match the following synonyms?

1) Migrant:

2) One who revolts:

3) Reorganize:

4) Disaster:

5) Flee:

3. Seek the words. Find the vocabulary words from the box below in the puzzle.

Humanitarian	Crisis	Unfolding	Forces	Escape
Fundamentalist	Alliance	Regroup	Internal	Refugees
Curfew	Partition	Rebel	Offensive	Heavily-armed
Militants	Casualty	Convoy	Overloaded	Civilians

Taliban Forces 2 Million to Flee														
F	U	N	D	A	M	E	N	T	A	L	I	S	T	H
P	U	O	R	G	E	R	C	Z	Y	Z	E	H	U	U
C	I	V	I	L	I	A	N	S	O	V	V	W	G	M
H	B	O	E	N	S	L	X	P	V	Z	I	E	S	A
O	E	B	X	U	O	F	K	R	N	S	S	T	I	N
A	E	A	A	G	N	I	D	L	O	F	N	U	N	I
R	L	L	V	N	E	S	T	V	C	A	E	I	T	T
I	T	L	N	I	I	E	E	I	T	B	F	C	E	A
Y	L	J	I	S	L	R	G	I	T	H	F	H	R	R
D	T	H	I	A	L	Y	L	U	E	R	O	J	N	I
E	Z	R	O	O	N	I	A	W	F	S	A	A	A	A
S	C	U	A	D	M	C	R	R	R	E	C	P	L	N
K	E	D	F	O	R	C	E	S	M	E	R	A	Q	O
W	E	F	R	U	C	V	A	T	I	E	E	E	P	C
D	F	B	Z	H	U	D	R	R	P	Y	D	S	M	E

Practice Makes Perfect

1. Read the following statements about the article. Answer true or false.

a) Millions of civilians have fled their homes to escape fighting in Pakistan.   T / F

b) The article says 2.5 million people in the Swat Valley are displeased.   T / F

c) The Pakistan Army has refused to lift a curfew to allow people to flee.   T / F

d) The recent refugee crisis is Pakistan's worst in many decades.   T / F

e) It seems the fighting is calming down a little.   T / F

f) A Pakistan newspaper reported the army is on the attack.   T / F

g) There are 10,000 more new Pakistani troops than Taliban fighters.   T / F

h) A Taliban spokesman said Pakistani army casualties were greater.   T / F

2. Match the following words or phrases with sentences from the article.

a) A new humanitarian crisis is

b) Hundreds of thousands of Pakistanis have

c) 900,000 civilians moved to avoid the

d) Cars and overloaded buses formed

e) The partition of India and

f) Fighting between the Pakistan military

g) They are increasing their efforts to root

h) The military went

i) A Taliban spokesman denied the

j) Pakistani troops killed just

1) a huge convoy

2) casualty figures

3) on the offensive

4) unfolding in Pakistan

5) out the militants

6) fled their homes

7) three Taliban soldiers

8) Pakistan accurred in 1947

9) violence

10) and Taliban rebels

3. With a partner, discuss the following humanitarian problems. How might you solve these issues for the Afghani refugees?

Problem	Your solution
Security	
Food	
Shelter	
Hope	
Health care	

NOTES:

Write On!

Free write for 10 minutes about war. Be creative! What words do you think of when you think of war? What kinds of problems cause war? Is war natural? What solutions do you have for peace? Is war ever good? Has war ever accomplished anything positive?

....

....

....

....

....

....

....

....

....

....

....

....

....

....

Phrasal Verbs

To make out

- I can make it out.
- I can't make out what he's saying.
- Can you make it out?

The Whole Story

Read these fascinating facts related to war and dispute.

War, Dispute and Bombs

① The shortest war on record took place in 1896 when Zanzibar surrendered to Britain after 38 minutes.

② Since 1495, no 25-year period on planet Earth has been without war.

③ In 1997, the US maintained 13,750 nuclear warheads, 5,546 of them on ballistic missiles.

④ In 1998, the US spent more than $35 billion on its nuclear weapons program.

⑤ In 1997, the US exported $15,6 billion in arms to developing countries, 54% of which went to non-democratic regimes.

⑥ Global spending on defense total more than $700 billion. Global spending on education is less than $100 billion.

⑦ There are 92 known cases of nuclear bombs lost at sea.

Unit
12

China vs. the Internet

Get Real!
Discussion and Debate
for English Language Learners

Unit 12

China vs. the Internet

⏻ **Themes and Topics**

- Censorship
- Pornography
- Internet safety

📂 **Vocabulary Preview**

Shut down	Contain	Pornographic	Crackdown
Material	Immoral	Content	Arrest
Focus	Reliable	Challenge	Long-term
Complex	Task	Distribute	Complaints
Uphill battle	Censor	Censorship	Campaign

Article

China Closes 1250 Pornographic Sites

The Chinese government has shut down around 1,250 Internet sites that contain pornographic material. It is the latest effort by China to crack down on immoral content. In addition to the crackdown, authorities have arrested 41 people involved in putting pornography online.

The deputy director of China's Internet Affairs Bureau, Liu Zhengrong, said the focus of the government's actions is to create a safer environment for children who use the Internet. Liu told reporters: "The campaign is aimed at creating a healthy Internet environment for all young people and making the Internet in China safer and more reliable." Liu outlined the difficulties ahead, saying: "Our biggest challenge is that the Internet is still growing... We are facing a long-term, complex and huge task."

In China it is illegal to distribute pornographic material. The Xinhua news agency reports that in the past three weeks the government has received more than 18,000 complaints about inappropriate content. Officials have also warned China's most popular sites, including Google and Baidu, to do more to block pornographic material from their searches in China. The task of censoring sites in China seems to be an uphill battle.

China has the largest online community in the world. There are almost 300 million users in China and this number is growing rapidly, at the rate of a quarter of a million a day. There are also 20,000 new sites uploaded to the Web every week. Many people fear the crackdown might also aim to censor news sites such as the BBC and Voice of America.

Discussion and Debate

1. Answer the following questions related to the article.

1) Is the Internet safer without the 1250 pornographic sites?

a Why or why not?

b Did China do the right thing?

c Is it the government's job to ban sites?

2) What are laws in your country about pornographic sites?

a Do these laws help make the Internet safer?

b Do these laws work?

c Is immoral or illegal material still available?

3) China, and other communist countries have a history of censorship:

a Is censorship of pornographic materials the same as censorship of religious materials?

b Why or why not?

c Do people have a "right" to access all kinds of information?

4) Does censorship benefit a society?

a What good can come of censoring information?

b Can society be safer?

c Can children be safer and more protected from immoral ideas?

d Does censorship lead to naivety?

5) Does access to information create a better society?

  a Which information makes society better?
  b What about censoring academic ideas?
  c What about censoring government secrets?
  d What is the difference between propaganda and censorship?

6) Do you think pornographic sites should be banned?

  a Why or why not?
  b What about parental controls?
  c What about just not visiting sites you don't like?

7) Whose job is it to stop "immoral" content on the Internet?

  a Our parents?
  b Lawmakers and government?
  c People who use the Internet?
  d Nobody?

8) What is healthy about the Internet?

  a E-mail?
  b Access to news and information?
  c Pictures?
  d Chatting?

9) What is unhealthy about the Internet?

  a Online gambling?
  b Chatting?
  c Rumors and gossip?
  d Pornography?

10) What are the biggest Internet dangers to children?

    a Seeing pornography?

    b Being lied to by people in chat rooms?

    c Becoming addicted to Internet games?

    d Becoming lazy and uninterested in sports?

NOTES:

Building Vocabulary

1. Review this list of vocabulary words. Translate the English words into Korean.

▶ English	▶▶ Korean	▶ English	▶▶ Korean
Shut down		Challenge	
Contain		Long-term	
Pornographic		Complex	
Crackdown		Task	
Material		Distribute	
Immoral		Complaints	
Content		Uphill battle	
Arrest		Censor	
Focus		Censorship	
Reliable		Campaign	

2. Match the following synonyms with vocabulary words from part 1.

1) Chore:

2) Close:

3) Difficulty:

4) Capture:

5) Corrupt:

```
Practice Makes
     Perfect
```

1. Read the following statements about the article. Answer true or false.

    a)   China has closed some sites about unhealthy eating and lifestyles. T / F

    b)   The government has arrested 41 people. T / F

    c)   The government wants a healthier online environment for kids. T / F

    d)   An official said the speed of the Internet's growth is a problem. T / F

    e)   The article said over 80,000 people complained to China's government. T / F

    f)   China has the world's largest number of Internet users. T / F

    g)   There are 250,000 new Chinese users going online every day. T / F

    h)   The article said China is going to crack down on the BBC and VOA. T / F

2. What do you know about the dangers of the Internet? Write the dangers of the following activities, and how we can stay safe online.

	Dangers	How to stay safe
Pornography		
Kids' sites		
Online banking		
Online shopping		
Cyworld		
Internet dating		

3. Match the following words or phrases with the best ending phrase from the article.

1)	sites that contain pornographic	a)	huge task
2)	crack down	b)	children
3)	create a safer environment for	c)	than 18,000 complaints
4)	making the Internet in China safer	d)	material
5)	a long-term, complex and	e)	of a million a day
6)	the government has received more	f)	to censor news sites
7)	an uphill	g)	on immoral content
8)	the largest online	h)	battle
9)	at the rate of a quarter	i)	and more reliable
10)	the crackdown might also aim	j)	community

4. Rate the following Web challenges from 1-8, 1 being the most important and 8 being the least important. What do you think is the most important challenge on the Web today?

_____ protecting personal information	_____ being online anywhere
_____ keeping kids from pornography	_____ credit card security
_____ Internet speed	_____ stopping online censorship
_____ keeping spam away	_____ staying safe on Cyworld

Write On!

Free write for 10 minutes about censorship. Be creative! What do you know about censorship in your country? What about in other countries? Is censorship good? Is it bad? Is it dangerous?

_____

_____

_____

_____

_____

_____

_____

_____

_____

_____

_____

_____

_____

_____

✎ Phrasal Verbs

To shut down

- I want to shut down the website.
- I want you to shut it down.
- Shut it down!
- What happens if the website shuts down?

The Whole Story

Read these fascinating facts about Internet safety.

8 Internet Safety Tips

- Never give out your personal information, your real name, address, or phone number, or any personal information about your family or friends without their permission.
- Be careful in chat rooms. Don't get involved in fights or use obscene language. You could be reported and have your internet service suspended or cancelled.
- If you are in a chat room and someone makes you feel uncomfortable, attempts to start a fight with you, or uses offensive language, leave the room.
- Ignore obscene or offensive messages. Replying may cause the sender to continue to send such messages.
- Be careful in joining mailing lists. Some may make your personal information public. Don't provide an address or phone number. The information for which you are signing up is sent to the e-mail address you provide, so they don't need your address or phone number.
- Beware of offers for free items, get-rich-quick offers or weight loss offers. They may be a scam.
- Beware of e-mail from people you don't know or e-mail you weren't expecting. It may contain a virus designed to damage your computer or send your account name and password back to the sender.
- Never send your picture to someone you don't know or trust. Remember, the internet allows people to become anyone they want to be, and they may be someone you don't really want to know.

References

"A Million Flee Pakistan-Taliban Fighting." Breaking News English 16 May 2009. 26 June 2009 <http://www.breakingnewsenglish.com/0905/090516-pakistan.html>.

"China Closes 1250 Sites for Healthier Web." Breaking News English 25 January 2009. 26 June 2009 <http://www.breakingnewsenglish.com/0901/090125- porno graphy.html>.

"Debunking the 9/11 Myths: Special Report". Popular Mechanics. March 2005. 22 June 2009 <http://www.popularmechanics.com/science/defense/1227842.html>.

Feuer, Alan. "500 Conspiracy Buffs Meet to Seek the Truth of 9/11". New York Times 5 May 2009. June 5 2006 <http://www.nytimes.com/2006/06/05/us/ 05conspiracy.html>.

"Google Software to Stop Drunken E-mails." Breaking News English 9 October 2008. 26 June 2009 <http://www.breakingnewsenglish.com/0810/081009-drunkenness.html>.

"Liquid Candy Needs Health Warnings." Breaking News English 15 July 2005. 26 June 2009 <http://www.breakingnewsenglish.com/0507/050715-soda-e.html>.

"Men Funnier than Women." Breaking News English 23 December 2007. 26 June 2009 <http://www.breakingnewsenglish.com/0712/071223-humor.html>.

"Men More Attracted to Women in Red." Breaking News English 30 October 2008. 26 June 2009 <http://www.breakingnewsenglish.com/0810/081030-colour. html>.

"New Study Says Coffee is Good for You." Breaking News English 29 August 2005. 26 June 2009 <http://www.breakingnewsenglish.com/0508/050829-coffee-e.html>.

"Traffic Pollution Damages Kid's Lungs." Breaking News English 2 February 2007. 26 June 2009 <http://www.breakingnewsenglish.com/0702/070202-pollution. html>.

Wikipedia Encyclopedia. 9/11 Conspiracy Theories. 23 June 2009 <http://en.wikipedia. org/wiki/9/11_conspiracy_theories>.

저/자/소/개

Myeong-Hee Seong

Ph.D., Korea University

Professor, Eulji University

Katie Mae Klemsen

MA, Monterey Institute of International Studies

Professor, Eulji University

Get Real!
Discussion and Debate for English Language Learners

2009년 8월 20일 인 쇄
2009년 8월 25일 발 행

저 자   Myeong-Hee Seong
         Katie Mae Klemsen

발행인   (寅製) 진 욱 상

발행처   백산출판사

서울시 성북구 정릉3동 653-40
   등 록 : 1974. 1. 9. 제 1-72호
   전 화 : 914-1621, 917-6240
   FAX : 912-4438
http://www.baek-san.com
edit@baek-san.com

저자와
합의하에
인지첩부
생략

값 **11,000 원**(CD포함)
ISBN 978-89-6183-221-2(93740)